TAILS from History

A Puppy for Helen Keller

By **May Nakamura**
Illustrated by **Rachel Sanson**

Ready-to-Read

Simon Spotlight

New York   London   Toronto   Sydney   New Delhi

SIMON SPOTLIGHT
An imprint of Simon & Schuster Children's Publishing Division
1230 Avenue of the Americas, New York, New York 10020
This Simon Spotlight edition December 2018
Text copyright © 2018 by Simon & Schuster, Inc.
Illustrations copyright © 2018 by Rachel Sanson
All rights reserved, including the right of reproduction in whole or in part in any form.
SIMON SPOTLIGHT, READY-TO-READ, and colophon are registered trademarks of Simon & Schuster, Inc.
For information about special discounts for bulk purchases, please contact Simon & Schuster Special
Sales at 1-866-506-1949 or business@simonandschuster.com.
Manufactured in the United States of America 1118 LAK
10 9 8 7 6 5 4 3 2 1
Library of Congress Cataloging-in-Publication Data
Names: Nakamura, May, author. | Sanson, Rachel, illustrator. Title: A puppy for Helen Keller /
by May Nakamura ; illustrated by Rachel Sanson. Description: New York : Simon Spotlight, 2018. | Series:
Tails from history | Series: Ready-to-read | Audience: Age 6-8. Identifiers: LCCN 2018001521 | ISBN
9781534429109 (hc) | ISBN 9781534429093 (pbk) | ISBN 9781534429116 (ebook) Subjects: LCSH: Keller,
Helen, 1880-1968—Juvenile literature. | Dogs—Anecdotes—Juvenile literature. Classification:
LCC SF426.5 .N35 2018 | DDC 636.7—dc23 LC record available at https://lccn.loc.gov/2018001521

In 1937, Helen Keller sailed
on a ship from America to Japan.
It was her very first time
traveling to Asia.

Helen Keller was a famous author who could not see or hear.
Helen traveled all around the world.
She shared her stories about learning how to read, write, and speak.
She inspired and helped many people.

A blind man named Takeo Iwahashi
(say: ta-KAY-o ee-wa-HA-shee)
had invited Helen to Japan.
Like Helen, he wanted to help
other people like him.
He printed many books in braille
(say: BRAYL) so that blind people
could read and learn.

The Japanese people loved
listening to Helen's speeches.
Helen spoke about peace,
respect, and understanding
other people's differences.

Helen also had a special request
while she was in Japan.
She wanted to meet
an Akita (say: ah-KEE-tuh) dog!

The Akita is a dog breed
from Japan.
Ever since she was a little girl,
Helen had loved dogs.
She had owned many dogs,
but she had never owned an Akita.

Helen had read about the true story
of the Akita named Hachikō
(say: ha-chi-KOH).
Every evening Hachikō met his
owner at the train station.
But one day Hachikō's owner
did not come home after work.

More trains came and left.
Hachikō waited and waited,
but his owner never appeared.

The next day Hachikō went
to the station again.
He went the next day, and the next.
For more than nine years
Hachikō didn't give up looking
for the person he loved.

Helen was inspired by Hachikō
and his loyalty.
She wanted to meet an Akita dog.
She met a small puppy
that she nicknamed "Kami"
(say: KAH-mee).

Kami licked Helen's cheek
and cuddled in her lap.
"May I keep him?"
Helen asked.
Kami's owner said yes!

Kami traveled with Helen
to his new home in New York.
He became the first Akita
to live in the United States.

But a few months later
Kami died from a virus
that affects some dogs.
Helen was very sad.

The Japanese people were also
sad to hear about Kami's death.
Kami had connected Helen to
Japan, but now he was gone.
The Japanese people had an idea.
They would send another dog
to Helen!

Kenzan-Go (say: ken-zahn-GO),
or "Go-Go,"
was Kami's brother.

Go-Go was bigger than Kami,
but he was just as friendly.
He would be the perfect fit
for Helen!

But there was a problem.
Trouble was brewing between
Japan and the United States.

Back in 1922 both countries had promised to stop building new battleships. They wanted to focus on peace, not war.

But as time went on,
Japan changed its mind.
It started building new battleships.

Americans were worried.
Japan's army and navy were growing.
The US president was not sure
if he could trust Japan.

Some people in Japan were scared
that Go-Go's trip would be unsafe.
No one knew what would happen
with all the trouble and distrust.

Go-Go was still ready
to meet Helen.
His ship left Japan
in the beginning of June 1939.

The journey was long and far.
Go-Go's ship was surrounded by
blue ocean and blue sky.

Finally the ship arrived in New York.

Would Go-Go be allowed off the ship?

"Welcome to America!"
the guard said.
And there was Helen Keller,
standing on the pier!

Go-Go ran to his new owner
and gave her a big doggy kiss.
Helen laughed.
They were so happy
to be with each other.

Helen was very grateful for the gift.
When Helen was with Go-Go,
she remembered all the kind people
she had met in Japan.

No matter what happened,
Helen would always think of
the Japanese people as her friends.
Go-Go lived a long and happy life
with Helen Keller.
Nothing could separate an
Akita and its owner.

· Facts About Akita Dogs ·

• Akitas are strong and powerful. They used to be popular hunting dogs!

• Akitas get their name from the Akita region in northern Japan.

• Akitas have webbed toes. This makes it easier for them to walk on snow.

• In Japan the Akita dog is considered a national treasure.

• Hachikō is still very famous today. Movies have been made and books have been written about his story. In Tokyo there is also a famous Hachikō statue at the Shibuya (say: shee-BU-ya) train station. The statue is a popular meeting spot.

· Facts About Helen Keller ·

• Helen Keller was born on June 27, 1880, and died on June 1, 1968.

• She became blind and deaf when she was nineteen months old.

• Helen was the first blind and deaf person to graduate from college.

• Helen traveled to Japan with her companion, Polly Thomson. One of the ways they communicated with each other was spelling words onto the other person's palm.

• Helen visited Japan again in 1948 and 1955.